THE JPS B'NAI MITZVAH TORAH COMMENTARY

Va-yikra' (Leviticus 1:1–5:26)
Haftarah (Isaiah 43:21–44:23)

Rabbi Jeffrey K. Salkin

T0326795

The Jewish Publication Society · Philadelphia
University of Nebraska Press · Lincoln

INTRODUCTION

News flash: the most important thing about becoming bar or bat mitzvah isn't the party. Nor is it the presents. Nor even being able to celebrate with your family and friends—as wonderful as those things are. Nor is it even standing before the congregation and reading the prayers of the liturgy—as important as that is.

No, the most important thing about becoming bar or bat mitzvah is sharing Torah with the congregation. And why is that? Because of all Jewish skills, that is the most important one.

Here is what is true about rites of passage: you can tell what a culture values by the tasks it asks its young people to perform on their way to maturity. In American culture, you become responsible for driving, responsible for voting, and yes, responsible for drinking responsibly.

In some cultures, the rite of passage toward maturity includes some kind of trial, or a test of strength. Sometimes, it is a kind of "outward bound" camping adventure. Among the Maasai tribe in Africa, it is traditional for a young person to hunt and kill a lion. In some Hispanic cultures, fifteen year-old girls celebrate the *quinceañera*, which marks their entrance into maturity.

What is Judaism's way of marking maturity? It combines both of these rites of passage: *responsibility* and *test*. You show that you are on your way to becoming a *responsible* Jewish adult through a public *test* of strength and knowledge—reading or chanting Torah, and then teaching it to the congregation.

This is the most important Jewish ritual mitzvah (commandment), and that is how you demonstrate that you are, truly, bar or bat mitzvah—old enough to be responsible for the mitzvot.

What Is Torah?

So, what exactly is the Torah? You probably know this already, but let's review.

The Torah (teaching) consists of "the five books of Moses," sometimes also called the *chumash* (from the Hebrew word *chameish*, which means "five"), or, sometimes, the Greek word Pentateuch (which means "the five teachings").

Here are the five books of the Torah, with their common names and their Hebrew names.

- **Genesis (The beginning), which in Hebrew is Bere'shit (from the first words—"When God began to create").** Bere'shit spans the years from Creation to Joseph's death in Egypt. Many of the Bible's best stories are in Genesis: the creation story itself; Adam and Eve in the Garden of Eden; Cain and Abel; Noah and the Flood; and the tales of the Patriarchs and Matriarchs, Abraham, Isaac, Jacob, Sarah, Rebekah, Rachel, and Leah. It also includes one of the greatest pieces of world literature, the story of Joseph, which is actually the oldest complete novel in history, comprising more than one-quarter of all Genesis.
- **Exodus (Getting out), which in Hebrew is Shemot (These are the names).** Exodus begins with the story of the Israelite slavery in Egypt. It then moves to the rise of Moses as a leader, and the Israelites' liberation from slavery. After the Israelites leave Egypt, they experience the miracle of the parting of the Sea of Reeds (or "Red Sea"); the giving of the Ten Commandments at Mount Sinai; the idolatry of the Golden Calf; and the design and construction of the Tabernacle and of the ark for the original tablets of the law, which our ancestors carried with them in the desert. Exodus also includes various ethical and civil laws, such as "You shall not wrong a stranger or oppress him, for you were strangers in the land of Egypt" (22:20).
- **Leviticus (about the Levites), or, in Hebrew, Va-yikra' (And God called).** It goes into great detail about the kinds of sacrifices that the ancient Israelites brought as offerings; the laws of ritual purity; the animals that were permitted and forbidden for eating (the beginnings of the tradition of kashrut, the Jewish dietary laws); the diagnosis of various skin diseases; the ethical laws of holiness; the ritual calendar of the Jewish year; and various agricultural laws concerning the treatment of the Land of Israel. Leviticus is basically the manual of ancient Judaism.

> Numbers (because the book begins with the census of the Israelites), or, in Hebrew, Be-midbar (In the wilderness). The book describes the forty years of wandering in the wilderness and the various rebellions against Moses. The constant theme: "Egypt wasn't so bad. Maybe we should go back." The greatest rebellion against Moses was the negative reports of the spies about the Land of Israel, which discouraged the Israelites from wanting to move forward into the land. For that reason, the "wilderness generation" must die off before a new generation can come into maturity and finish the journey.

> Deuteronomy (The repetition of the laws of the Torah), or, in Hebrew, Devarim (The words). The final book of the Torah is, essentially, Moses's farewell address to the Israelites as they prepare to enter the Land of Israel. Here we find various laws that had been previously taught, though sometimes with different wording. Much of Deuteronomy contains laws that will be important to the Israelites as they enter the Land of Israel—laws concerning the establishment of a monarchy and the ethics of warfare. Perhaps the most famous passage from Deuteronomy contains the *Shema,* the declaration of God's unity and uniqueness, and the *Ve-ahavta,* which follows it. Deuteronomy ends with the death of Moses on Mount Nebo as he looks across the Jordan Valley into the land that he will not enter.

Jews read the Torah in sequence—starting with Bere'shit right after Simchat Torah in the autumn, and then finishing Devarim on the following Simchat Torah. Each Torah portion is called a parashah (division; sometimes called a *sidrah,* a place in the order of the Torah reading). The stories go around in a full circle, reminding us that we can always gain more insights and more wisdom from the Torah. This means that if you don't "get" the meaning this year, don't worry—it will come around again.

And What Else? The Haftarah

We read or chant the Torah from the Torah scroll—the most sacred thing that a Jewish community has in its possession. The Torah is written without vowels, and the ability to read it and chant it is part of the challenge and the test.

But there is more to the synagogue reading. Every Torah reading has an accompanying haftarah reading. Haftarah means "conclusion," because there was once a time when the service actually ended with that reading. Some scholars believe that the reading of the haftarah originated at a time when non-Jewish authorities outlawed the reading of the Torah, and the Jews read the haftarah sections instead. In fact, in some synagogues, young people who become bar or bat mitzvah read very little Torah and instead read the entire haftarah portion.

The haftarah portion comes from the Nevi'im, the prophetic books, which are the second part of the Jewish Bible. It is either read or chanted from a Hebrew Bible, or maybe from a booklet or a photocopy.

The ancient sages chose the haftarah passages because their themes reminded them of the words or stories in the Torah text. Sometimes, they chose *haftarah* with special themes in honor of a festival or an upcoming festival.

Not all books in the prophetic section of the Hebrew Bible consist of prophecy. Several are historical. For example:

The book of Joshua tells the story of the conquest and settlement of Israel.

The book of Judges speaks of the period of early tribal rulers who would rise to power, usually for the purpose of uniting the tribes in war against their enemies. Some of these leaders are famous: Deborah, the great prophetess and military leader, and Samson, the biblical strong man.

The books of Samuel start with Samuel, the last judge, and then move to the creation of the Israelite monarchy under Saul and David (approximately 1000 BCE).

The books of Kings tell of the death of King David, the rise of King Solomon, and how the Israelite kingdom split into the Northern Kingdom of Israel and the Southern Kingdom of Judah (approximately 900 BCE).

And then there are the books of the prophets, those spokesmen for God whose words fired the Jewish conscience. Their names are immortal: Isaiah, Jeremiah, Ezekiel, Amos, Hosea, among others.

Someone once said: "There is no evidence of a biblical prophet ever being invited back a second time for dinner." Why? Because the prophets were tough. They had no patience for injustice, apathy, or hypocrisy. No one escaped their criticisms. Here's what they taught:

> God commands the Jews to behave decently toward one another. In fact, God cares more about basic ethics and decency than about ritual behavior.
> God chose the Jews *not* for special privileges, but for special duties to humanity.
> As bad as the Jews sometimes were, there was always the possibility that they would improve their behavior.
> As bad as things might be now, it will not always be that way. Someday, there will be universal justice and peace. Human history is moving forward toward an ultimate conclusion that some call the Messianic Age: a time of universal peace and prosperity for the Jewish people and for all the people of the world.

Your Mission—To Teach Torah to the Congregation

On the day when you become bar or bat mitzvah, you will be reading, or chanting, Torah—in Hebrew. You will be reading, or chanting, the haftarah—in Hebrew. That is the major skill that publicly marks the becoming of bar or bat mitzvah. But, perhaps even more important than that, you need to be able to teach something about the Torah portion, and perhaps the haftarah as well.

And that is where this book comes in. It will be a very valuable resource for you, and your family, in the b'nai mitzvah process.

Here is what you will find in it:

> A brief **summary** of every Torah portion. This is a basic overview of the portion; and, while it might not refer to everything in the Torah portion, it will explain its most important aspects.
> A list of the **major ideas** in the Torah portion. The purpose: to make the Torah portion real, in ways that we can relate to. Every Torah portion contains unique ideas, and when you put all

of those ideas together, you actually come up with a list of Judaism's most important ideas.

> Two ***divrei Torah*** ("words of Torah," or "sermonettes") for each portion. These *divrei Torah* explain significant aspects of the Torah portion in accessible, reader-friendly language. Each *devar Torah* contains references to **traditional** Jewish sources (those that were written before the modern era), as well as **modern** sources and quotes. We have searched, far and wide, to find sources that are unusual, interesting, and not just the "same old stuff" that many people already know about the Torah portion. Why did we include these minisermons in the volume? Not because we want you to simply copy those sermons and pass them off as your own (that would be cheating), though you are free to quote from them. We included them so that you can see what is possible—how you can try to make meaning for yourself out of the words of Torah.

> **Connections:** This is perhaps the most valuable part. It's a list of questions that you can ask yourself, or that others might help you think about—any of which can lead to the creation of your *devar Torah*.

Note: you don't have to like everything that's in a particular Torah portion. Some aren't that loveable. Some are hard to understand; some are about religious practices that people today might find confusing, and even offensive; some contain ideas that we might find totally outmoded.

But this doesn't have to get in the way. After all, most kids spend a lot of time thinking about stories that contain ideas that modern people would find totally bizarre. Any good medieval fantasy story falls into that category.

And we also believe that, if you spend just a little bit of time with those texts, you can begin to understand what the author was trying to say.

This volume goes one step further. Sometimes, the haftarah comes off as a second thought, and no one really thinks about it. We have tried to solve that problem by including a **summary** of each haftarah, and then a mini-sermon on the haftarah. This will help you learn how these sacred words are relevant to today's world, and even to your own life.

All Bible quotations come from the NJPS translation, which is found in the many different editions of the JPS TANAKH; in the Conservative movement's *Etz Hayim: Torah and Commentary;* in the Reform movement's *Torah: A Modern Commentary;* and in other Bible commentaries and study guides.

How Do I Write a *Devar Torah?*

It really is easier than it looks.

There are many ways of thinking about the *devar Torah.* It is, of course, a short sermon on the meaning of the Torah (and, perhaps, the haftarah) portion. It might even be helpful to think of the *devar Torah* as a "book report" on the portion itself.

The most important thing you can know about this sacred task is: *Learn* the words. *Love* the words. Teach people what it could mean to *live* the words.

Here's a basic outline for a *devar Torah:*

"My Torah portion is (name of portion) _____,
    from the book of _____ , chapter
    _____.

"In my Torah portion, we learn that_____
    (Summary of portion)
"For me, the most important lesson of this Torah portion is (what
    is the best thing in the portion? Take the portion as a whole;
    your *devar Torah* does not have to be only, or specifically, on the
    verses that you are reading).
"As I learned my Torah portion, I found myself wondering:
    ➤ *Raise a question that the Torah portion itself raises.*
    ➤ *"Pick a fight"* with the portion. Argue with it.
    ➤ *Answer a question* that is listed in the "Connections" section of
       each Torah portion.
    ➤ *Suggest a question to your rabbi* that you would want the rabbi
       to answer in his or her own *devar Torah* or sermon.

"I have lived the values of the Torah by _____
(here, you can talk about how the Torah portion relates to your
own life. If you have done a mitzvah project, you can talk about
that here).

How To Keep It from Being Boring
(and You from Being Bored)

Some people just don't like giving traditional speeches. From our per-
spective, that's really okay. Perhaps you can teach Torah in a different
way—one that makes sense to you.

> Write an "open letter" to one of the characters in your Torah por-
  tion. "Dear Abraham: I hope that your trip to Canaan was not too
  hard . . ." "Dear Moses: Were you afraid when you got the Ten
  Commandments on Mount Sinai? I sure would have been . . ."
> Write a news story about what happens. Imagine yourself to
  be a television or news reporter. "Residents of neighboring cities were horrified yesterday as the wicked cities of Sodom and
  Gomorrah were burned to the ground. Some say that God was
  responsible . . ."
> Write an imaginary interview with a character in your Torah portion.
> Tell the story from the point of view of another character, or a mi-
  nor character, in the story. For instance, tell the story of the Garden of Eden from the point of view of the serpent. Or the story
  of the Binding of Isaac from the point of view of the ram, which
  was substituted for Isaac as a sacrifice. Or perhaps the story of
  the sale of Joseph from the point of view of his coat, which was
  stripped off him and dipped in a goat's blood.
> Write a poem about your Torah portion.
> Write a song about your Torah portion.
> Write a play about your Torah portion, and have some friends act
  it out with you.
> Create a piece of artwork about your Torah portion.

The bottom line is: Make this a joyful experience. Yes—it could
even be fun.

The Very Last Thing You Need to Know at This Point

The Torah scroll is written without vowels. Why? Don't *sofrim* (Torah scribes) know the vowels?

Of course they do.

So, why do they leave the vowels out?

One reason is that the Torah came into existence at a time when sages were still arguing about the proper vowels, and the proper pronunciation.

But here is another reason: The Torah text, as we have it today, and as it sits in the scroll, is actually *an unfinished work*. Think of it: the words are just sitting there. Because they have no vowels, it is as if they have no voice.

When we read the Torah publicly, we give voice to the ancient words. And when we find meaning in those ancient words, and we talk about those meanings, those words jump to life. They enter our lives. They make our world deeper and better.

Mazal tov to you, and your family. This is your journey toward Jewish maturity. Love it.

THE TORAH

❖ Va-yikra': Leviticus 1:1–5:26

Hard as it might be to imagine, traditionally Leviticus was the first book of the Torah that Jewish children learned. That is how important it is—a handbook of what "Judaism" was like for the ancient Israelites.

This first Torah portion of Leviticus focuses, specifically, on the various kinds of sacrifices (*korbanot*) that the ancient Israelites brought to the *mishkan*, the ancient Tabernacle in the desert (and, after that, the Temple in Jerusalem). Each kind of sacrifice had its own purpose, and those purposes can help us understand exactly what motivated the ancient Israelite worshiper to want to approach God. The sacrifices were not for God; they were ways to elevate the individual and to help the individual in his or her quest for holiness.

Summary

> God tells Moses about the sacrificial offerings (*korbanot*) that are to be offered. (1:1)
> Sacrificial offerings should come from either the herd or the flock. (1:2)
> But not all sacrifices need come from the herd or the flock; the worshiper can also bring birds and grain as offerings. (1:14–2:16)
> Worshipers can also bring a *zevach shelamim,* an offering of well-being, of *shalom.* (3:1–17)
> And they can bring a *chattat* offering, an offering that expresses regret for sin. The Torah speaks of two ways of understanding sin: what happens *if* a "regular" person sins, and what happens *when* a leader sins. (4:1–35)

The Big Ideas

> **Sacrifices were a way for the ancient Israelite worshiper to get close to God.** That is the meaning of the word *korban*. It comes from the Hebrew root *k-r-v*, which means "to get close." Worship, in whatever form it takes, is a way of achieving some kind of intimacy with God.

> **The sacrifices came from the herd or the flock—which means from domesticated animals.** In an ancient agricultural society, the most important things that the worshiper owned were animals. Animals, like sheep, goats, or cattle, were almost like money. To offer an animal meant that you were offering something that had real value.

> **Bird and grain offerings were the "economy" sacrifice.** Not everyone could afford to bring offerings like sheep, goats, or cattle; they were simply too valuable. So the sacrificial system allowed for less-expensive alternatives: birds and grain. Burning grain smells good, not so burning feathers, but to God those burning feathers smelled just fine. God cares about the dignity of the poor. Everyone has a role in Jewish life.

> **A major part of sacrificial offerings—and all worship—is being grateful for shalom.** That was the purpose of the *zevach shelamim*—to express gratitude for a sense of being at peace with your family, with the priests in the Tabernacle, and with God.

> **Everyone sins sometimes, but rulers and leaders are almost guaranteed to sin.** This is not only a statement about human nature (after all, no one is perfect). It is not only a cynical statement about how power corrupts. It is also a statement of absolute realism: it is almost impossible to be a leader without making mistakes. The best leaders are those who are able to own up to their errors, apologize, and then do things better.

Divrei Torah

IS THIS GOD'S BARBECUE?

Yuck. That's probably what you're thinking about this Torah portion, and maybe the entire book of Leviticus. Bringing animals to the altar and killing them, and then burning them? Who would do such a thing?

Well, actually, what do you think happens when you order meat in a restaurant? True, you don't actually kill the animal on the spot. No, you don't—but someone else slaughtered that animal before it showed up in the restaurant. So, unless you're a vegetarian, don't think that the ancient sacrifices were that disgusting.

But why did Judaism have to have animal sacrifices in the first place? The great medieval philosopher Maimonides suggests that it was necessary because this was what the Jews had experienced in Egypt: "God could not expect us to utterly abandon this mode of worship, for that would have gone against human nature. God therefore allowed these practices to continue but transformed them from idolatrous associations . . . that their purpose should be directed toward Him."

So, God was like a patient teacher, trying to move the Jews away from pagan sacrifice to making offerings for God. Maimonides understood that the ideal form of serving God was prayer, but it took some time for the Israelites to get there.

But on the way to that goal, did sacrifice have anything to teach the Jews?

Yes. We can learn something from the animals that are required as sacrifices. They are all domesticated animals; you have to bring what belongs to you. Those animals are not up in the mountains somewhere. God only asks the possible from us, not the impossible.

What kinds of animals are required? Oxen, sheep, and goats. Each animal is the prey of another animal. The ox is pursued by the lion, the sheep by the wolf, the goat by the leopard. In this way, the sages thought that God was telling the ancient Israelites that many nations would pursue them as well. That was their way of learning what their future history would be.

But what does it really mean to sacrifice? Rabbi David Wolpe writes: "In every relationship, part of the measure of love is the willingness to forgo; I will sacrifice sleep, food, time, money, almost anything for someone whom I love. In ancient Israel, offering the products of labor—crops, animals—showed deep connection to God." So, were the sacrifices disgusting? Maybe.

Did they have something to teach? Definitely.

WHEN LEADERS SIN

It happens. It will always happen. Rulers sin. They make mistakes, sometimes terrible mistakes.

Sure, we know all about the horrible leaders, the tyrants and killers like Hitler, Stalin, Idi Amin, Saddam Hussein, and others. But what about the good leaders? Moses, the greatest leader the Jews ever had, killed a man in Egypt. King David, the true founder of the kingdom of Israel and the greatest king in the Bible, killed a man and then stole his wife. Many American presidents, like Franklin Roosevelt, Dwight Eisenhower, John F. Kennedy, and Bill Clinton, were sometimes unfaithful to their wives. Sometimes political leaders make even worse mistakes—like waging wars that turn out to be less than absolutely necessary.

Judaism understands that this sort of thing happens. Look at what Leviticus says about the sin offering that sinners have to bring. When it comes to "regular" people, the text says "if a person sins." *If.* It might happen; it might not (it probably does, because no one is perfect). But when it comes to rulers, Leviticus does not say *if* they sin. It's *when* they sin. It is going to happen. Be ready for it. As the talmudic sage Yochanan ben Zakkai said: "Fortunate is the generation whose leader recognizes having sinned and brings an offering of purification."

And here is what is even cooler: Biblical Judaism brought a radical revolution to political thinking: the ruler is not above the law. In ancient times, and in non-Jewish nations, if you criticized the ruler you could get yourself killed. The ruler or king was a god. But when King David sinned, the prophet Nathan stood before him and openly criticized him. When King Ahab and Queen Jezebel sinned, the prophet Elijah stood before them and openly criticized them. That was what prophets were supposed to do. True, it didn't win them any popularity contests. And it was also true that it was dangerous; Elijah had to flee from Queen Jezebel, who threatened to kill him. But here's the bottom line: no prophet in ancient Israel was ever put to death by a king for telling the truth to the king.

The Israeli statesman Avraham Burg writes: "The role of the prophet and man of spirit is to stand always at the side of the oppressed and downtrodden, the 'average citizen,' and defend him or her against an unjust regime. Our tradition understands that there is no government that is without injustice."

Connections

➤ Why do you think that Jewish children used to start their Jewish education by learning the book of Leviticus?

➤ Why does Leviticus make special mention of the sins of rulers? What would be some examples of those kinds of sins?

➤ How does Judaism show concern for the dignity of the poor? How do you yourself do this?

➤ For what are you grateful? How do you show your gratitude?

➤ What kinds of offerings do you "bring" to God?

➤ What are your ways of getting close to God?

THE HAFTARAH

❖ Va-yikra': Isaiah 43:21–44:23

To review: there are two biblical prophets named Isaiah. The first was a prophet who lived in the eighth century BCE. Then, there was a prophet who was called Second Isaiah. That wasn't actually his name (no one ever called him Isaiah 2). He was actually an anonymous prophet who preached during the sixth century BCE at the time when the Babylonian exile was about to end. (Sometimes, he is called Deutero-Isaiah; "deutero" means "repeat.") Everything in the book of Isaiah that comes after chapter 40 is the work of this anonymous prophet. (Some scholars say that there was even a third Isaiah, but we won't get into that now.)

The Second Isaiah was perhaps the most optimistic prophet in Jewish history. And why wouldn't he be? He felt sure he was about to witness one of the great moments in history—the coming return of the Jews to their homeland. His messages were always about hope.

According to Isaiah, God is upset that the Jews haven't brought offerings to God (that's the connection with the Torah portion Va-yikra', which is all about the sacrificial system), and haven't remembered their ethical obligations. No doubt, many Jews turned to the worship of Babylonian gods, and the prophet finds that both stupid and upsetting.

But then Isaiah's tone radically changes. Hey, Jews! We can reestablish our relationship with God! It's time to come home! We can do it!

What's Wrong with Idolatry, Anyway?

If there is one thing that made the prophets go ballistic, it was idolatry. Worshiping false gods is prohibited in the Ten Commandments. Over and over again, the Torah condemns those who worship the gods of ancient Canaan. The prophets hammer that message home: idolatry is bad.

But what was really so wrong about idolatry? Was it simply the worship of gods who didn't happen to be Adonai? Was it the worship of many gods, rather than the one true God? Was it the kind of worship that those false gods demanded—human sacrifice and other disgusting, terrible things? Or was there something much more basic?

The prophets objected to idolatry for all the reasons above, and we find an additional reason in this haftarah. Several times, the prophet known as Second Isaiah goes on a rant against those who make idols. "The makers of idols all work to no purpose; and the things they treasure can do no good, as they themselves can testify" (44:9). That's his biggest issue with idolatry: It's the issue of what the idolater worships! He or she is worshiping an object that someone created. And even if the idol is symbolic of some god, it's preposterous to bow down to an object itself.

Oh, sure, the craftsman who made the idol was very good at his or her work, and the prophet even gives credit where credit is due: "The craftsman in iron, with his tools, works it over charcoal and fashions it by hammering, working with the strength of his arm" (44:12).

But the prophet also has to laugh at that workmanship. Let's say that the idol maker uses a tree to make a wooden idol. The craftsman uses part of the tree to make the idol, and the other part of that same tree simply as firewood to use for roasting meat! How "holy" could the wooden god actually be, then?

You probably already know the famous legend about how thirteen-year-old Abram (Abraham) broke the idols that his father had made. "Abram seized a stick, smashed all the images, and placed the stick in the hand of the biggest of them. When his father came, he asked: 'Who did this to the gods?' Abram answered: 'A woman came with a bowl of fine flour and said: "Here, offer it up to them." When I offered it, one god said, "I will eat first," and another said, "No, I will eat first." Then the biggest of them rose up and smashed all the others.' His father replied: 'Are you messing around with me? They cannot do anything!' Abram answered: 'You say they cannot. Let your ears hear what your mouth is saying!'" Young Abram figured out that if you make something, that means you actually have power over it. And if you have power over something, then that "something" cannot be a god. Because you created it, it is actually a part of you.

Rabbi Ed Feinstein teaches: "An idol is . . . a projection of my desires, my fears, my needs. . . . So . . . I flatter and sweet talk the idol. I bring gifts to the idol and I beg the idol to do what I need done in the world. And if the idol complies, I become its loyal servant. And if not, . . . I'll shop my needs around until I find a god who's interested in helping me in exchange for my devotion. Cosmic room service."

That's why idols cannot be gods. Because they are simply projections of our own desires. So idolatry is a form of self-worship. And God is always much bigger than that.

❖ Notes